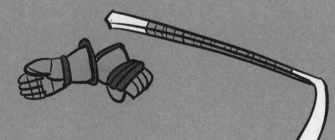

Sports Illustrated KIDS

MY FIRST BOOK OF HOCKEY

By Beth Bugler and Mark Bechtel

A ROOKIE Book

Illustrations by Bill Hinds

Hockey is a fast-moving game played between

TWO TEAMS.

The object of the game is to score more goals than the other team.

Goals are scored by shooting the

PUCK--->

with a stick into the other team's

NET.----->

This is **MY** net, and nothing's coming in here!

The **GOALIE** stands in front of the net. He wears extra pads and a catching glove to help stop the puck. Plus, he gets to wear a scary **MASK.**

So far, my mask would only scare a dentist.

In addition to the goalie, each team has three

FORWARDS,

the **left wing**, **center**, and **right wing**, who try to score goals.

The main job of the two

DEFENSEMEN

is to keep the other team from scoring.

Hockey is played on an ice

RINK

that's surrounded by walls called

BOARDS.

The ice is divided by five lines.

GOAL
LINE

BLUE
LINE

CENTER
RED LINE

BLUE
LINE

GOAL
LINE

The game is played in

THREE PERIODS

that are **20 MINUTES** each.

That means we have **TWO SNACK BREAKS!**

Okay, the players are on the ice,
the fans are fired up, it's time for the . . .

...FACE-OFF!

The referee drops the puck
between the two centers,
and they each try to control
it with their stick.

Swoosh! The center flicks the puck over to his teammate, who makes a

PASS

up the ice.

He better get this, or I'm not passing to him again.

Look out! The player with the puck is

CHECKED

by an opponent, who tries to knock him away from the puck!

It's times like these I'm glad I'm a ref.

Yikes. Maybe I'll look into figure skating.

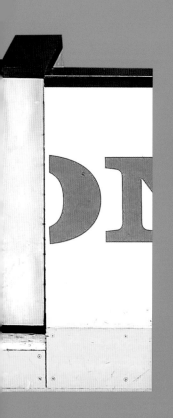

A player is on the ice for a short period of time, called a

SHIFT.

When he gets tired, he'll skate to the bench and a teammate will replace him. This can happen

ON THE FLY,

which means right in the middle of a play!

TIME

6:45

Nope! The goalie stopped the puck from going into the net. That's a

SAVE!

The first period ends.
Boy, is the ice surface scratched
up! The players leave the rink
and on comes the

ZAMBONI

to smooth the ice over.

Can you save some
of those ice shavings
for my snow cone?

The second period begins
with another face-off.

Slap! Scrape! Whoosh!
The center flies down the ice,
past the defenders for a

BREAKAWAY.

He's one-on-one with the goalie. He shoots . . .

PERIOD

2

After the face-off, the referee blows his whistle.

Uh-oh!

A player hit an opponent above the shoulders with his stick. That's high-sticking, and it's a

PENALTY.

Now he has to go sit in the

PENALTY BOX

for two minutes.

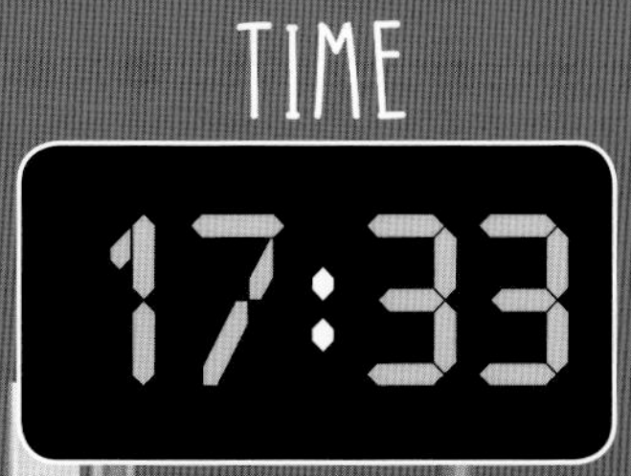

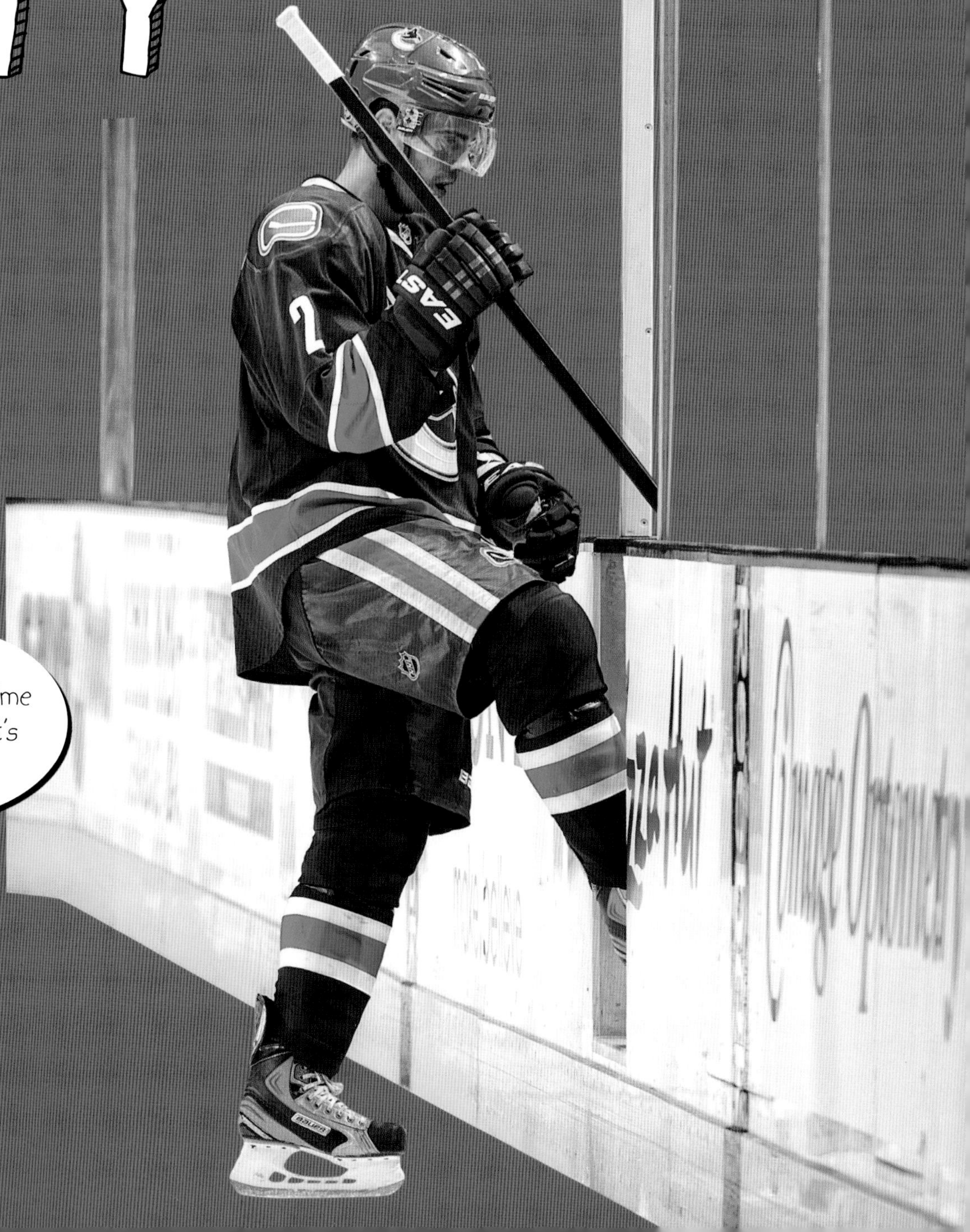

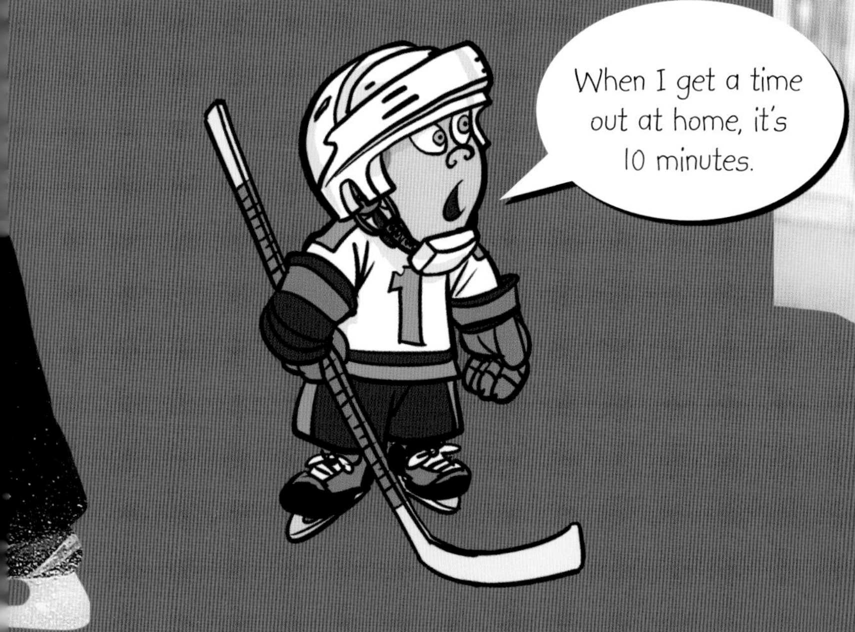

While the player is in the penalty box, the other team has an advantage called a

POWER PLAY.

They now have five skaters on the ice, while the other team only has four.

Hey! Want to make it five and a half?

These are some other no-nos.

INTERFERENCE

When a player gets in the
way of another player who
doesn't have the puck

HOLDING

When a player grabs
another player and
doesn't let go

This is Mom's signal for when I mess up.

SLASHING

When a player swings his stick at another player and hits him

HOOKING

When a player tries to stop an opponent by snagging him with the curved part of his stick

The power play is over, and the teams are back to five-on-five. The defenseman is under pressure. He just wants to get the puck away from his goal.

Helloooooooooooo!

He sends it all the way down the ice. If it goes from his side of the center line to the other team's goal line, that's

ICING.

The play is stopped, and the puck is brought back down the ice for a face-off.

So this isn't about cupcakes?

The horn signals the end
of the second period.

Time to clean the ice again!

Another face-off and the game continues. Oops! A player has skated over the blue line toward the other team's goal **BEFORE** the puck crossed the line.

The goalie makes a save, but the puck bounces off his glove. A forward pounces on the

REBOUND

and sends it into the net. GOAL!

It's the player's **third goal** of the game. That's called a

HAT TRICK,

and the fans throw their hats onto the ice to celebrate.

Sweet! I've been looking for a red hat!

OVERTI

But I'm so tired!

Five more minutes
are put on the clock.
Instead of five skaters,
each team uses three.
The first team to
score wins.

Writers: Mark Bechtel, Beth Bugler
Designer: Beth Bugler
Illustrator: Bill Hinds
Production Manager: Hillary Leary

Copyright © 2016 Time Inc. Books

Published by Liberty Street, an imprint of
Time Inc. Books
225 Liberty Street
New York, New York 10281

ISBN 13: 978-1-61893-177-1
Library of Congress Control Number: 2016937899

First edition, 2016

2 TLF 17

10 9 8 7 6 5 4 3

To order Time Inc. Books Collector's Editions,
please call (800) 327-6388, Monday through Friday,
7 a.m.-9 p.m., Central Time.

We welcome your comments and suggestions
about Time Inc. Books.
Please write to us at:
Time Inc. Books
Attention: Book Editors
P.O. Box 62310
Tampa, FL 33662-2310
(800) 765-6400

timeincbooks.com

Time Inc. Books products may be purchased for
business or promotional use. For information on bulk
purchases, please contact Christi Crowley in the
Special Sales Department at (845) 895-9858.

Printed in China

PHOTO CREDITS, in order
Graig Abel/NHLI/Getty Images (title page);
Bill Smith/NHLI/Getty Images (left team);
Jana Chytilova/Freestyle Photography/Getty Images
(right team); Jared Wickerham/NHLI/Getty Images
(goalie); Brian Babineau/NHLI/Getty Images (mask);
Bill Smith/NHLI/Getty Images (forwards, defensemen);
Tim Smith/Getty Images (rink); Andre Ringuette/
NHLI/Getty Images (face-off); Bruce Kluckhohn/
NHLI/Getty Images (pass, 2); Michael Martin/NHLI/
Getty Images (checked); Victor Decolongon/Getty
Images (shift); Andrew Dieb/Icon Sportswire/AP
(slap shot, 3); Jared Silber/NHLI/Getty Images
(save, 2); Jamie Squire/Getty Images (Zamboni); Norm
Hall/NHLI/Getty Images (breakaway goalie); Aaron
Poole/NHLI/Getty Images (breakaway shooter); Jamie
Sabau/NHLI/Getty Images (goal); Jeff Vinnick/NHLI/
Getty Images (penalty, penalty box); Christian
Petersen/Getty Images (power play); Doug Pensinger/
Getty Images (interference); Graig Abel/NHLI/Getty
Images (holding); Andy Marlin/NHLI/Getty Images
(slashing, hooking); Rebecca Taylor/NHLI/Getty
Images (defensemen); David Hahn/Icon Sportswire/AP
(icing); Len RedKoles/NHLI/Getty Images (Zamboni);
Jeff Vinnick/NHLI/Getty Images (referee); Gregory
Shamus/NHLI/Getty Images (offsides, 2); Rich Lam/
Getty Images (goalie); Elsa/Getty Images (rebound);
Jared Silber/NHLI/Getty Images (hat trick); Norm
Hall/NHLI/Getty Images (hats); Victor Decolongon/
Getty Images (overtime); Dave Sandford/NHLI/Getty
Images (game over); Jonathan Kozub/NHLI/Getty
Images (back cover)